W9-BWX-070

Chicago Public Library
North Pulaski Branch
4300 W. North Ave.
Chicago, IL. 60639
(312) 744-9573
Mon., Wed., Fri., & Sat.:9am-5pm
Tues. & Thurs.:12pm-8pm Sunday:Closed

Formas: rectángulos
Shapes: Rectangles

Chicago Public Library
North Pulaski Branch
4300 W. North Ave.
Chicago, IL. 60639
(312) 744-9573
Mon., Wed., Fri., & Sat.:9am-5pm
Tues. & Thurs.:12pm-8pm Sunday:Closed

Esther Sarfatti

Rourke
Publishing LLC
Vero Beach, Florida 32964

EASY Sp QA 482 .S35818 2008
Sarfatti, Esther.
Formas.

© 2008 Rourke Publishing LLC

All rights reserved. No part of this book may be reproduced or utilized in any form or by any means, electronic or mechanical including photocopying, recording, or by any information storage and retrieval system without permission in writing from the publisher.

www.rourkepublishing.com

PHOTO CREDITS: © Nicole S. Young: title page; © Dragan Trifunovic: page 5; © Viorika Prikhodko: page 7; © Renee Brady: page 9; © Jody Dingle: page 11; © Graeme Mowday: page 13; © Bonita Hein: page 15; © Jeroen Peys: page 17; © Eva Serrabassa: page 19; © Marzanna Syncerz: page 21; © Vladimir Kondrachov: page 23.

Editor: Robert Stengard-Olliges

Cover design by Nicola Stratford.

Library of Congress Cataloging-in-Publication Data

Sarfatti, Esther.
Shapes : rectangles / Esther Sarfatti.
p. cm. -- (Concepts)
ISBN 978-1-60044-526-2 (Hardcover)
ISBN 978-1-60044-667-2 (Softcover)
1. Rectangles--Juvenile literature. 2. Shapes--Juvenile literature. I. Title.
QA484.S268 2008
516'.154--dc22
2007014074

Printed in the USA

CG/CG

Rourke Publishing

www.rourkepublishing.com – rourke@rourkepublishing.com
Post Office Box 3328, Vero Beach, FL 32964

R03243 11816

Chicago Public Library
North Pulaski Branch
4300 W. North Ave.
Chicago, IL. 60639
(312) 744-9573
Mon., Wed., Fri., & Sat.:9am-5pm
Tues. & Thurs.:12pm-8pm Sunday:Closed

Esto es un rectángulo.
This is a rectangle.

Hay rectángulos por todas partes.

Rectangles are everywhere.

Los libros son rectángulos.

Books are rectangles.

Esta puerta es un rectángulo.

This door is a rectangle.

Este carrito es un rectángulo.

This wagon is a rectangle.

Esta piscina es un rectángulo.

This swimming pool is
a rectangle.

Esta cama es un rectángulo.

This bed is a rectangle.

Este juego tiene rectángulos.

This game has rectangles.

Estos regalos son rectángulos.

These presents are rectangles.

Este cajón de arena es un rectángulo.

This sandbox is a rectangle.

Hay rectángulos por
todas partes.
¿Puedes encontrar
los rectángulos?

Rectangles are everywhere.
Can you find the rectangles?

Índice

carrito 10
libros 6
puerta 8
regalos 18

Index

books 6
door 8
presents 18
wagon 10

Lecturas adicionales / Further Reading

Leake, Diyan. *Finding Shapes: Rectangles*. Heinemann, 2005.
Olson, Nathan. *Rectangles Around Town*. A+ Books, 2007.

Páginas Web recomendadas / Recommended Websites

www.enchantedlearning.com/themes/shapes.shtml

Acerca de la autora / About the Author

Esther Sarfatti lleva más de 15 años trabajando con libros infantiles como editora y traductora. Ésta es su primera serie como autora. Nacida en Brooklyn, Nueva York, donde creció en una familia trilingüe, Esther vive actualmente en Madrid, España, con su esposo y su hijo.

Esther Sarfatti has worked with children's books for over 15 years as an editor and translator. This is her first series as an author. Born in Brooklyn, New York, and brought up in a trilingual home, Esther currently lives with her husband and son in Madrid, Spain.